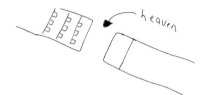
heaven

this book

...is for those who struggle
with self-doubt and the constant,
impossible pursuit of perfection
and for those who anguish over
idealism and concerns about
how others perceive them.

the essential luxury of you
offers insight + inspiration
for how to gain self-confidence,
embrace flaws, and claim happiness.
filled with sketches + evocative poems,
the essential luxury of you
encourages readers to release
the weight of insecurity in their
pursuit of self-development and
instead to celebrate themselves
and the imperfections that make
them beautiful and unique.

The Essential Luxury of You:

Visual Reminders
to Dismantle Self-Doubt
and Learn to Celebrate You

Cassandra Campbell Stanley

ISBN 9781457564444

Printed in USA by 48HrBooks (www.48HrBooks.com)

thank you, mama, aunty, and aunt murl, for showing me the indomitable
strength of a woman and the awe-inspiring power of faith.
fierce, feisty, courageous and unapologetic.
my example. my reason.

to my husband, my rock, my mirror, my laugh, and my reminder.

to my sister friends, you're so damn fly. you are my home.

to my little cousin swann, you're the future, past and present.
i wrote this for you.

to the family who chose me. you raised me
and loved me unconditionally.

to all who saw magic in me when i didn't always see it in myself.

to anyone who has to learn and relearn on a daily basis
that you are enough and you belong, i see you. i am you.

let light shine, always and in all ways.

xo,
cass

chapter 1

REFLECT

1

chapter 2

REALIZATION

15

chapter 3

GROWTH

51

chapter 4

PEACE

77

chapter 5

GOALS

103

chapter 6

YOU

127

chapter 7

REPEAT

155

xo,
Cassie

Chapter 1
REFLECT

dear friend,

i'm glad you found this note.

let me tell you what this book is all about.

it's a visual collection of my "note to self" moments and the lessons i've learned (so far) while on my whirly and winding journey from chronic self-doubt to learning how to celebrate who i am (even the messy parts).

i have an educator's heart and the spirit of a perpetually curious student, so admittedly, i wrote this book in part to serve as a vault of notes that i could constantly revisit when i questioned my worth and needed to relearn these lessons. admittedly, these moments happen often since i'm still figuring all this out. i seem to unlearn and relearn the same truths all the time. i also knew that i wasn't the only person who struggled with honoring their worth and learning to celebrate every fiber of their being, not just the pieces that are shiny and bright. since we are one another's keepers, consider this book an act of "passing my notes," just in case you ever need a little inspiration, encouragement, or a simple reminder that you're not alone and want to study life's lessons together.

in sharing this book with my hand-drawn scribbles, my intention is to remind you of a few truths:

1. the pictures i drew aren't perfect; they're not meant to be, and neither are you. messy and imperfect are just right. you're amazing because of the mess—that's the strength of your beauty!

2. you can still be in the midst of a journey while sharing lessons learned. too often, we tell ourselves, "i will earn the right to share my story *only* when i'm completely out of this part." while writing this book, i confronted the idea that i didn't have a right to share the lessons i've learned because i'm still learning them. yet i discovered that learning how to celebrate who you are is a lifelong journey with new and interesting layers that are revealed over time. the journey,

to me, is a journey that i can arrive at daily, moment by moment, and the time to share the lessons learned is now.

3. your story is your own. sharing your story unlocks power, intimacy, courage, and beauty, and the first person who should sit with and unpack your story … is you! writing this book allowed me to own my story more fully and get even more curious about the source of my perceptions, behaviors and habits. i had to face my fear of judgment and being misunderstood or labeled and replace it with courage. by bringing the truth of my experiences into the light, i could begin to bask in the warmth of healing. this book is an act of defiance against self-doubt, insecurity, and shame and an invitation for others to find their act of defiance … after all, we're in this together!

4. all the tools you need to be who you want to be are right in front of you. i drew each of these pictures on long bus rides home from work using the notes section on my phone and my index finger. that's it.

5. you don't always have to be classically trained to start doing what you want. oftentimes, passion, scrappiness, hard work, incessant curiosity, clear intention, and *faith* will fill the gap between here and way, way, waaaay over there. i wanted to write a book, so i wrote a book. who is it that you want to be? what is it that you want to do? if there is something that you're extremely curious about trying, an offering you really want to make to the world, or a secret dream you want to pursue but are too scared or complacent to start, be scared and find a way to do it anyway. don't wait for permission; you don't need it. and if you're still waiting for permission, well, permission granted!

6. we have more in common than we realize. i hope that you'll be able to relate to parts of my story and can identify times when you may have experienced similar thoughts or feelings. when we share our stories, particularly the less savory parts, we reclaim the power they have, and we can reshape and redirect that power to serve a greater good—

honoring ourselves and building authentic connection and community with others.

too often, intrinsic, unapologetic joy is a luxury for a few when it should be a right for all.

you deserve to enjoy who you are, all of you. i hope this book makes you think, pause, smile, and want to celebrate who you are (imperfections, failures, and all), because you are worthy of your own friendship. you are an essential luxury.

> *okay, this first section was the appetizer, so if you have a short attention span and like pictures more than words, stop here and skip ahead to dive into the main course. i won't judge!*

> *for those of you still with me, let's get to know one another a little bit better and chat about the second puberty and how perfectionism, insecurity, and self-doubt became the insidious sidekicks i never wanted.*

my second puberty and my discoveries

have you ever heard of the "second puberty"? well, yeah, me neither, but as i transitioned from my twenties into my thirties, a shift started to happen, an internal stirring of sorts. growth and change in the deepest sense were brewing, and the best way i can describe it is that i had started my second puberty. although i'm pretty certain that *second puberty* is not an official scientific or psychological term, it's the perfect label, since this phase had all the signs of puberty.

check all that apply:

- ☐ being a little awkward and slightly alarmed about what the heck is going on
- ☐ seeking to find your place and where you belong
- ☐ oscillating between knowing and unknowing
- ☐ letting go of what you've outgrown (practices, behaviors, and clothes alike)
- ☐ embracing new (and rediscovered) elements of who you are
- ☐ gaining a deeper appreciation of what feeling at home in your own skin means and requires
- ☐ clearly recognizing that you are transforming and shifting into a new chapter of you

yup, i checked all of the above! by my own definition, i had all the signs of a second puberty. in every part of my being, i felt like i was being called to another phase of me. a rite of passage was occurring, and two discoveries, among many, stood out.

firstly, i discovered that it's easy to subscribe to the allure of perfection and connect it to your worth and personal ethos. and unbeknownst to me, at a very early age, i subscribed. perfectionism can manifest itself in different ways. for me, it takes the form of:

- anxiously and incessantly thinking that i'm not enough and not meeting expectations; self-confidence fueled mainly by external validation.
- obsessively mapping out my *x*-year plan a, b, and c while struggling to embrace and celebrate the present.
- muting and quieting parts of myself to fit in, belong, and be agreeable—hiding in plain sight.
- placing unrealistic pressure on myself to always be happy and suppress negative feelings.
- constantly second-, third-, fourth-guessing myself and losing precious time and energy because of the paralyzing fear of making the wrong decision and squandering an opportunity.
- keeping an idea safely tucked away in my head and procrastinating its execution to protect me from judgment and from incurring the looming (and somewhat debilitating) disappointment when the outcome and execution look nothing like how they looked in my mind. perfectionism tells me, "it's not going to turn out the way you want, and everyone's going to judge you for how crappy it is—don't bother or procrastinate until people forget what you said you were going to do." fantasizing about who i want to be and what i want to do, rather than actually doing it, keeps my most precious dreams in the realm of perfection and away from failure. perfectionism cradles the softest parts of me that can easily be bruised by the harsh and pretentious judgment of others.

secondly, i also discovered that high self-awareness doesn't mean high self-esteem and confidence. i know it sounds like a contradiction, but i'm proof that this, my friend, is not a contradiction at all! i knew i was caring, smart, honest, genuine, ambitious, and all these other yummy things, yet i constantly questioned if who i was and what i did were valuable and good enough (and it was sooooooooooo exhausting). i was constantly trying to be better and do better, comparing myself to others, comparing myself to the version of me i had fantasized about (you know, that version that says by the time i'm this age, i'll be and have this, that, and the other). i struggled with the jealousy that comparison spawns. i negotiated with myself to meet the standard of *enough* on a daily basis. if i do this, then i'll be *enough*. if i do that, then i'll be *enough*, but the bar to being *enough* always felt out of reach; it was always a moving target. by always focusing on improvement, i barely slowed down to truly enjoy myself. unapologetically basking in the *joie de moi*, the joie de vivre (mess and all), rarely made it to my to-do list.

it became increasingly clear that i was on the corner of sinister self-doubt and major insecurity, wearing the finest version of perfectionism i could find, and i wanted the directions out of it all. i had so many questions and was profoundly curious about my state of affairs. *how the heck did i get here, and how the heck do i get out? why do i struggle with celebrating who i am? why is it a challenge to stay present? why do i constantly feel like i'm not enough? why do i minimize or shy away from sharing my story?* i wanted the dna of my doubt, the origin of my self-consciousness and insecurity. this was a matter of identity. i sensed that to get *through*, i'd have to go *into* my story and reverse engineer my coordinates. it was going to get a little messy and uncomfortable. here's what i found.

an origin story: how achievement became the only part of my identity that mattered

i am first generation born in america of caribbean descent and come from a generation of women who had very humble beginnings. my great-aunt and grandmother had elementary school–level educations and worked most of their lives as domestics, cleaning other people's homes and raising other people's children. my mother and aunts grew up in kingston, jamaica, in a two-bedroom cinder block home with an unlit kitchen and bathroom that could only be accessed by walking outside across a dirt pathway. i was very aware of the sacrifices that were made for me to have better opportunities. they wanted me to go further with the weighted baton that they carried, and they hoped that it would be lighter for me. there was a palpable pressure to succeed, to make something of their sacrifices. i internalized the pressure and it intensified. it wasn't enough to just do well—no, not at all. to avoid squandering their sacrifice, i needed to be as close to perfect as possible. education and achievement were my vehicles to perfection.

i didn't need to look far for reminders of multigenerational sacrifices and motivation for high achievement and perfectionism. as a seven-year-old with a necklace that bore three keys hidden under my clothes, every day after school, i let myself into my apartment and was greeted by an empty home and a reminder that my parents were working to create a better life for me. after a separation from my dad, my single mom worked two jobs to help me pay for college, moonlighting her career as a special victims detective to work twelve-hour shifts as a security guard at a bank. with my family's sacrifices at the forefront of my mind, when it came to education and achievement, my priority from an early age was to work hard, not to necessarily have fun!

in my world, we didn't frivolously talk about the future—we had to have a plan! questions like "what do you like to do?" or "what brings you joy?" were questions of luxury that we simply couldn't afford. instead, the key question was "what job is the most secure?" although my aunt is extremely artistic, my great-aunt killed it in the kitchen, and my mom has an eye for fashion, the pursuit of security greatly eclipsed the pursuit of joy. granted, they did an amazing job at finding purpose in their secure careers, but it was always clear that the priority for them and for me needed to be security. doctor, lawyer, teacher, or nurse—those were the career paths i could choose from. scholastic and professional achievement became fiercely linked to my identity. whistling while i worked and enjoying the present was always muted by the fear that i would let everyone down, that i would drop the baton that was given to me by generations before me that never had the whisper of an opportunity to do anything close to what i was doing. the fear and anxiety that i would squander the chance because i didn't say the right thing, make the right career path decision, or maximize an opportunity was a sweeping undercurrent in my daily life. it wasn't a shout as much as it was like an insidious and annoying tune i couldn't get out of my head, a ringing in my ear that i was forced to get used to, or the sound of static from a television in another room while i was trying to rest. it kept me on edge, kept me on my toes, coloring my being, my disposition, and my world. the soundtrack of anxiety and fear was the background music to my life, and it was on repeat.

while i've always believed that success was failure turned inside out and that i could learn from every mistake, i also believed that there was little room to entertain missteps—the stakes were too high. although i had an inner rebel, a passionate provocateur that would run free, barefoot, unashamed and unapologetically, this side of me took the back seat to my desire to be accepted, to live up to others' expectations, and to avoid causing disappointment. in my child's mind, to err felt dangerous—there was too much at stake and too many who had paid a price for the opportunities that i was afforded. i was constantly being corrected and edited and corrected again for how i was and who i was. i molded and blended to avoid criticism. i ferociously sought out ways that i could do more and be more, and i obsessed over whether i was doing (and being) enough—i craved the external validation and acceptance. this singular obsession over striving to always be good enough, to always be better, to always do more became embedded in my fibers and showed up in less-than-rewarding ways as an adult. the same thought process that fueled my achievement was also poisoning me. over time, the false guise and security of achievement unraveled. plans were not working out as planned—i was achieving more and more, but i wasn't any happier with who i was. in fact, it was becoming increasingly clear that celebrating elements of who i was outside of achievement was foreign to me and something i was going to have to learn.

an origin story: insecurity with a side of suppression and distrust

there are so many aspects of my childhood that i look back on fondly, but there were troubling experiences that would shape my sense of security and level of trust in others. when i was a child, during a formidable time in life when people develop a sense of trust in the world and the people around them, when they seek security and predictability as firm ground in developing their identities, seeds of insecurity, defensiveness, anxiety, and distrust were planted in my psyche. i was surrounded by love, but on a deeper level, i never felt 100 percent secure. i learned very early that life can be very unpredictable and i needed to keep my guard up in defense of its' unpredictable nature. i felt like things were happening to me and around me and there was little i could do about it. my sense of agency and control felt thwarted and defensiveness and a general sense of distrust took their place. my biological father unexpectedly (and rather suddenly) passed away when i was two years old. i would sob in school because i missed him. it didn't seem fair that i would not remember my time with him. i'd tearfully hold my few pictures of him, mourning a person i looked like but would never know. when i was four, while attending my grandmother's church, a man old enough to be my grandfather molested me—he lured me with candy and a smile and would be my first kiss. every so often someone will walk by bathed in his faint yet distinct scent and i instantly remember him. i knew the precarious nature of loving someone who's health was extremely fragile and stigmatized by society. i also grew up with a person very close to me that had a less-than-healthy relationship with alcohol and lived in the world of lies, unfaithfulness, insecurity, drama and silent shame this relationship breeds. my mom and step-father (the person i call "dad") were both detectives in the new york police department. as an occupational hazard, they were gruesomely reminded on a daily basis that the world is dangerous and i, in turn, adopted a deeply rooted understanding of this danger. the fear of unexpected death loomed over my childhood. as early as i can remember, in case something suddenly happened to my mom, she would remind me of where all the "important life papers" were in the house, and for years, my only nightly prayer was for God to bring her home safely. i started doing laundry solo in the first grade because my parents thought it was important for me to have a sense of independence—anything could happen to them and i needed to be prepared.

i was desperate to find a way to regain control, so i found my own ways of coping. in my child's mind, this is how i saw the world – since my parents can die at any moment and unsuspecting people can take advantage of me and try to hurt me when i least suspect it, i needed to stay alert, to be aware, to not take things at face value and to read in between the lines. this perspective gave me a sense of control but heightened my anxiety. i tried to anticipate outcomes based on previous experiences as a means to protect myself from getting hurt. i became overanalytical, defensive and sensitive as a means of survival and protection. i also came to recognize that some of this behavior was generational – lessons of "hope for the best but expect the worse" and "trust no one" were passed down because of the world that my mom had to live in and the traumas she experienced. every time my hyper-vigilance yielded an answer that proved correct, confirmed an instinct or successfully revealed someone's ill intent, my will to protect myself grew stronger… but my will to survive was coming at a cost.

i continued to seek the security i so desperately wanted in all the wrong places. i sought friendships with people who tolerated and teased me behind my back, rather than celebrating me. i would compromise myself for others' approval—feeling ashamed, like something was wrong with me when i didn't fit in. food was my go-to security blanket; every indulgent bite gave me a false, but oh so real, sense of peace. during my pivotal adolescent years, when my sense of identity was ripe for development, i chose to be in a long-term relationship with someone who was *very* manipulative and critical of me, always finding something about me that needed to change—i was never enough just as i was. this further fueled my insecurities.

the other way i coped with feelings of powerlessness, anger, sadness, and fear growing up was to internalize, suppress, and minimize the truth and impact of my reality. "it could always be worse, right?" i wanted to find the bright side so i didn't have to deal with the darkness. before having hard, heart-to-heart, and sensitive conversations, i often withdrew and retreated into isolation as a way of processing negative emotions. sometimes i was defensive as a way of protecting the softest and most insecure parts of me. having experienced moments when people used my insecurities to put themselves on pedestals over me or to label me with a scarlet letter that i couldn't shake and criticized me (most often as whispers behind my back), i struggled with trusting people with my insecurities. i didn't want to willingly hand them over to be judged. so i kept my messy parts, memories, past, and situations to myself.

what i came to know too well was that the cocktail of silence, denial, and suppression mixed with insecurity and a bit of an identity crisis is a very slippery slope into anxiety, depression, and dark, unmentionable thoughts that i was desperate to quiet. i so desperately wanted some peace. it was painful and scary to fully own and accept my entire story, and over time, i learned that minimizing the most formative parts of my story had some unintended side effects. apparently, when you don't fully and unconditionally own who you are and what you've experienced, mess and all, the only other enticing option is to doubt yourself (*go figure!*). so, unintentionally, i invited self-doubt, self-consciousness, and insecurity to make themselves at home.

an origin story: quieting parts of myself

as a black woman who was often in rooms, large and small, where i was the only one (or one of a few) in mostly white spaces, i became hyperaware of my own existence and presence. when you're the only, oftentimes you're not fully present in any given experience, and you're double-minded—you're living the experience and you're also the witness to the experience, processing the implications of situations as they happen. i became intimately familiar with the beauty and pain of being the only in a room. when you've been the only in a room and there's an emotional and spiritual charge associated with it—in other words, you were deeply impacted and moved by the experience in some way—your general empathy level for others grows exponentially. you develop an instinct to try to make others feel like they belong. you seek ways to celebrate others, to make them feel comfortable and unjudged because you never want them to question themselves. you're thrown into the deep end of the pool of relationships, and you're either going to sink (remain isolated and disconnected) or swim (find ways to genuinely connect and develop rapport). when you're the only, you learn how to truly be curious about others and lean into this curiosity with ease, seeking out your commonalities, because when you're the only, what you have in common with the dominant culture may not always be so obvious. you also learn how to join conversations and worlds that are unlike your own with a certain level of grace, openness, kindness, and humillity—there's little room for self-righteousness, ego, or being judgmental. when you're the only, you become more proficient in the language of humanity and connection.

there's also a painful and isolating side of being the only, where identity and belonging are put into question. i was constantly in circles and environments where everyone seemed more similar than not—where lifestyles, experiences, personalities, and interests mirrored one another. where conversations were about topics that sounded like a foreign language. where the six degrees of separation was more like two degrees—many were one person away from a shared acquaintance or friend. where social capital and currency were subconsciously exchanged and negotiated through a slew of shared experiences and paradigms—"i like you because you're a lot like me." where the benefit of the doubt, tolerance, and patience were more generously offered to the similar, and psychological safety seemed to be built with greater ease when like was among like. where you learned the difference between inviting someone to the party and accepting them. the unintended message a homogeneous culture sends is that if you don't fit this mold, then you don't belong—"we're right, and you're wrong." it was very easy to feel like an outsider looking in. there was a whole other layer of self-consciousness. i spent a lot of daily mental, emotional, and spiritual headspace reminding myself that i was worthy of a seat at the table—i belonged.

there's a famous maya angelou quote, one of my favorites: "i go forth alone and stand as ten thousand." it recognizes all the people who came before me, that paved the way for me to be in the room, who couldn't be in the room, who didn't have the choice. it's one of my greatest sources of strength. there's also a certain level of responsibility that i honor that can lead to an overwhelming and distracting level of pressure. i am not oblivious to what it means when i'm in a room. i've felt a pressure that i'm representing my entire culture, being mindful not to feed into stereotypes. i had to be mindful of what i do and say and how i did and said things and even how i looked. i stand at five feet ten inches and know that my physical presence alone can feel imposing to others. if i'm not smiling or not jovial or if i say something too directly or in the wrong tone, i may get labeled as agressive or the angry black woman with an attitude. thoughts like *don't ruffle feathers, be grateful that you're even in the room* often cross my mind, and these thoughts manifest themselves as constantly being self-censored, toning myself down and making myself smaller to make others feel more comfortable. instead of just saying what i needed to say, i often second-guessed myself and was hesitant—*did i say that right? was that too harsh? was that agreeable enough?* historically, black people were conditioned to be subservient, to submit and be passive, to prioritize others' comfort over our own. these generational chains of oppression and mental and emotional enslavement are deeply rooted and sometimes barely recognizable. it took me a while to realize how these chains were showing up in my life.

i've questioned whether my hair was "too black" for a job interview and if my outfit read "too urban." i learned what my mother meant when she said that i had two strikes against me: "you're black, and you're a woman—you're going to have to work harder." the margin for error seemed narrower for me than my peers, and the level of effort it took for me to be at the exact same table was different. i saw that i couldn't get away with the same level of ease and general carefreeness that i saw my peers had or i would fall a beat behind. when you're the only in a room, privilege becomes clear. it's a privilege not to question your existence in a space. it's a privilege to feel laid-back and carefree in an environment that tells you that who you are is celebrated. it's a privilege to feel completely comfortable, able to bring your whole self to a space without hesitation, question, self-consciousness, or need to code switch. it's a privilege to never wonder if you're there to fill a quota. it's a privilege to just be.

the irony is that we live in a society that, in macro and micro ways, marginalizes people of color on a daily basis. sometimes it whispers "you are inferior" so quietly and consistently that it can feel normal and creep into your unconscious. it picks at, borrows, recreates, glorifies and appropriates the parts of our culture deemed worthy and won't acknowledge that we are the source of inspiration because to do so would validate our beauty. it tells us that we're not good enough, minimizes our existence, history and contributions. it attempts to muffle our power and sometimes erase us all together. yet we're called to be confident in ourselves, to not doubt ourselves, to not feel self-conscious, to not be sensitive, to get over it! then we're judged and labeled when we're not and don't. if you are in an environment that tells you that you're wrong in subtle and overt ways, you can quiet aspects of yourself that don't fit into the cultural archetype. i so desperately wanted to be understood but didn't always know how to explain the nuances of my experience, so i internalized them. over time, i started to shut down because to open up and spotlight my differences to a group whose members seemed to be mirrors of one another felt much lonelier than just sitting alone. over time, my friendly, warm, and endearing disposition began to erode and give way to frustration, disillusionment, and sadness—it was becoming too much. you compromise parts of yourself to fit in, and it becomes a slippery slope—what else are you willing to give up in order to fit in and belong? what other behaviors are you willing to do to belong? you quiet so many parts of you until you fall silent and are unrecognizable, even to yourself. i learned, the painful way, that you can't quiet aspects of yourself and celebrate who you are at the same time. i was going to have to choose—and i chose me!

an origin story: the essential luxury of you

this book is a defiant act of healing. it was birthed from the fact that i no longer wanted to hide in plain sight. i wanted to embrace my story and my life unapologetically, without shame. i was developing the practice of accepting and finding value, beauty, and texture in both the light and the darkness. my experiences sparked resilience and made me more compassionate for others and empathetic to the silent pain that people carry on a daily basis and the various ways it shows up. however, some of the behaviors, perceptions and habits that i developed while processing these experiences were no longer serving me. i wanted more for myself. i wanted to embrace a new chapter of me. i wanted to reclaim the power that these circumstances and experiences had over me. it was time to reprogram how i processed my life. i would have to change the orientation in which i engaged with my past, present and future. i'd have to refocus on the truth that every hurt, every mess, every struggle was designed for me and could be used for a greater purpose, but that would be completely up to me. it would be a daily practice, a second-by-second practice. some days simply suck, while others feel like i'm in my groove—but it's all worthy of celebration because it's my journey. this is a journey with a destination at which i can arrive daily, and the destination is my truest self.

we talk about loving and celebrating ourselves, but what does that really mean? to me, to celebrate who you are is to embrace who you are, to own who you are, to place yourself in your own hands, to stand on the side of you. to revel in your own company. to find delight in yourself. to be your own friend and confidant. to dwell in a place of joy, honor, trust, and respect for yourself. it means to take the time, to find your practice, to protect, to honor, to learn and relearn the sacredness of you. to approach yourself with patience, forgiveness, and kindness.

it's easy for some of us to lose ourselves in the minefield of self-doubt, shame, insecurity, anxiety, depression, withdrawal, pain, sadness, frustration, and more. i get lost, and i've had to find myself more times than i can count. it's a daily, active, and intentional practice to find myself again and again. it's also easy for some of us to question our belonging, our worth, and our value. this book is a reminder that we are required, we are necessary, we are needed, we are essential (yes—those are all synonyms, but it's so important i need to say it in every way i can). we should revel, embrace, bask in, cherish, learn about, delight in, and honor every detail of who we are—you are worthy of your own time.

a lot of love and attention went into making you, so consider this book an invitation for you to find new ways to enjoy and delight in yourself—to see the essential luxury of you.

xo,
cass

Chapter 2
REALIZATION

your life is your story to write.

you can't control what happens to you, but your response and interpretation, well, that's all you, babe!

you can rewrite the story to reveal the veiled lessons.

others can only have the pen if you give it to them.

get out of your head.

get out of your own way.

the present has your name on it.

have unapologetic tunnel vision about the kind of person you want to be.

be prepared for distractions and necessary rerouting.

make loving who you are and loving others (without exception) a part of your vision.

the internal tape that plays on repeat in your mind shapes how you see everything.

be diligent, meticulous, and precise about the content on the tape.

sometimes it feels like you're sitting in traffic watching everyone drive at full speed in the opposite lane. *yes, you're going in the right direction; keep your eyes on the road.*

sometimes it feels like your gps has you driving in circles. *a familiar road means there's a deeper lesson to uncover.*

sometimes it feels like you've been driving for hours. *no, you didn't miss your exit (i promise).*

move and shake at your own damn pace.

go at the speed of you and don't miss the view.

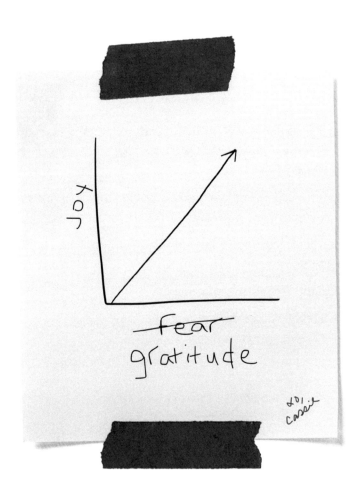

yup, i'm scared of pure joy.

a bit paranoid perhaps.

what happens when it goes away?

what will i do if i lose it?

do i even deserve it?

gratitude is the antidote.

there's a time for absolution.

then there's gray.

gray is for consideration.

gray questions the status quo.

gray asks why and why not?

gray listens, observes, analyzes, and embraces.

gray reserves judgment.

gray creates space.

gray pauses.

gray waits.

there's a time for absolution.

then there's gray.

be curious.

there's an adventure to be had.

lust after wonder.

get lost.

find the self that was there in the beginning.

that was there all along.

there's a magnetic pull between you and the ship with your name on it.

the shore may be familiar, but your adventure awaits.

don't watch your ship sail.

ant, a three-letter word for *masterful teacher.*

humbly make your offering.

believe in its significance, no matter how small.

move and act with intention and purpose.

serve others.

serve something greater than yourself.

nature nurtures the human spirit.

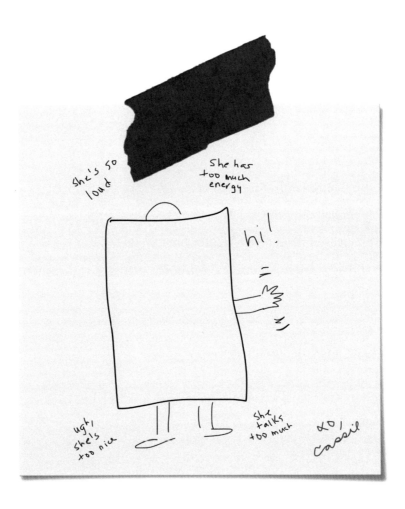

hiding from gossip only blocks your view.

unburden yourself.

don't take it personally.

there's so much world to see, wouldn't want you to miss it.

it's all about perspective.

who holds more weight for you?

there may be more people who think you're nothing special, let it be a reminder to cherish those who uplift you.

go where it feels like sunshine.

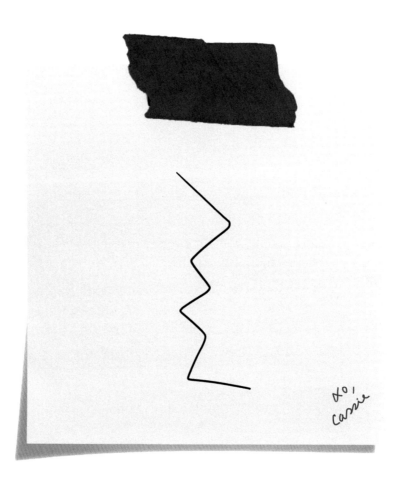

split.

break.

she asked me—what kind of conversations do you want to have?

gossip.

taints.

she asked me—what kind of conversations do you want to have?

hurt others.

hurt yourself.

she asked me—what kind of conversations do you want to have?

judge others.

miss the story.

she asked me—what kind of conversations do you want to have?

build.

destroy.

she asked me—what kind of conversations do you want to have?

conversations create …

we are creators.

split decisions.

break the chain.

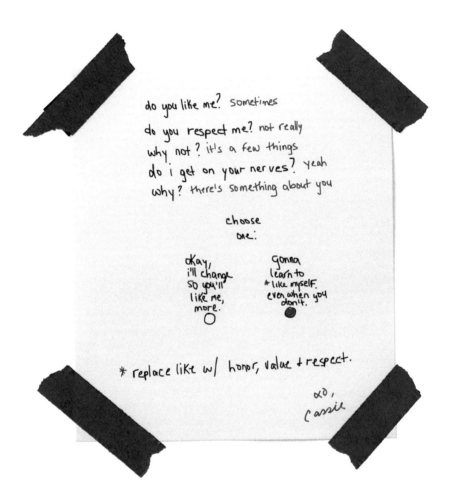

i bend for your acceptance.

i move for your acknowledgment.

i ask for your permission.

i change my temperature if you're uncomfortable.

i question myself if you question me.

i don't like me when you don't like me.

i let your story of me dictate my story of myself.

i get quiet if you think i'm too loud.

i turn down if you think i'm too turned up.

i wonder if i fit.

i wonder how to fit.

i wonder if i can fit

what if i stopped …

and started to do for myself what i was asking you to do for me—
celebrate me unconditionally.

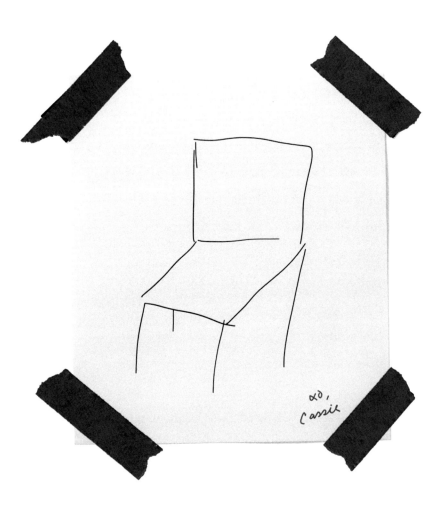

find your seat.

you don't have to prove your worth.

sit.

find your table.

no table?

make one.

you have a right to both.

i hold this truth to be self-evident.

some silently and not so silently judge you.

to your face.

behind your back.

some whisper. some text. some type.

yet they're only saying what you say to yourself.

some find pleasure in highlighting your insecurities.

some are masters of hiding their own.

they seem to have the kind of insecurities that sit peacefully at the dinner table. eating all their vegetables, asking to help wash the dishes afterward.

confidence?

my insecurities seem to eat with their mouths open, clothes stained with sauce, food stuck in their teeth, not a utensil in sight, crumbs everywhere, napkins—who needs them?

disaster.

insecurities on front street.

insecurities exposed.

what does this dot mean?

    a.   you're exactly where you should be.

    b.   life always sends you messages with common themes.
          look for them.

    c.   this dot can mean whatever you want it to mean. you have
          control over how you see and interpret everything.
          such is life.

    d.   maybe i just wanted you to slow down enough to stare
          mindlessly at a random-ass dot.

    e.   all of the above.

Chapter 3
GROWTH

oh, wait, so growth isn't instantaneous?

damn it, that's not what the commercial said!

and . . .

xo,
Cassie

a dangerous elixir, when inspiration mixes with crippling self-doubt.

you know which one i'm talking about? the doubts imbued with *too, never, don't,* and *supposed to.*

the thieves of joy, surprise, and delight.

the self-imposed barriers that come from comparison.

it's too late, and …

i'm not _____ enough, and …

i missed my chance, and …

i'm supposed to have_____ and i don't have it, and …

i'll never be good at that, so why even try? and …

i'm too scared, and …

do it anyway.

be it anyway.

don't want me to pass me by.

what a delicious treat to indulge in the pleasure and surprise and mystery of me. of you.

ellipses through life.

some people may not get your dance moves.

they may stare in confusion and judgment.

that's okay.

they're allowed to stare.

you're allowed to keep dancing.

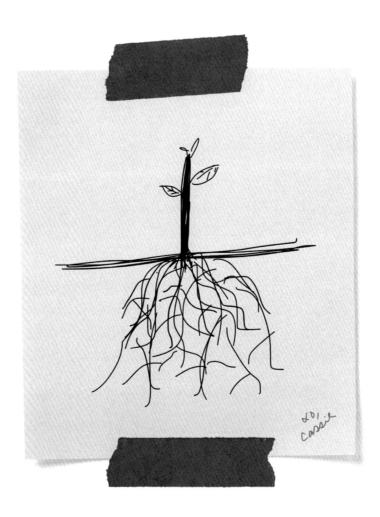

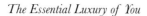

growth happens below the surface.

the beautiful network of everything that makes you who you are, those roots run deep.

yup.

always will be.

you miss a lovely truth when you compare yourself to others.

we're all gallivanting through life with bunched-up socks in our shoes.

it's the state of human affairs.

let's encourage one another to toss our shoes and walk barefoot in the sand.

damn, that feels good.

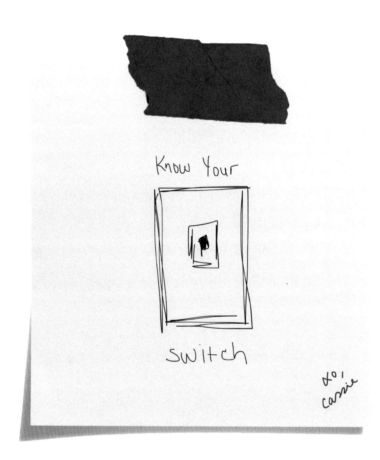

learn to love the lessons they teach.

this, my friend, is the human condition.

sometimes we judge others for what they're not doing, what they are doing, or what we think they should be doing. we offer to help them from a position of self-righteous judgment—which isn't really help at all, is it?

be mindful of the harshness of this judgment.

you're always one decision away from being the kind of person you'd rather not be.

one moment away from being in a situation you'd never thought you'd be in.

being kind to others is a rebellious and merciful act of self-love.

do it often.

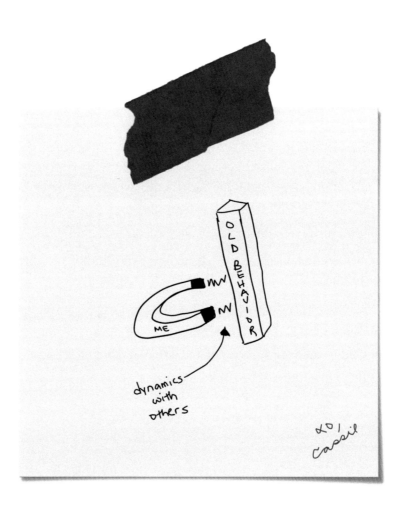

sometimes the hardest thing about evolving is people seeing, treating, and interacting with you in the same ways.

they consistently put you in "that" box because that's the only way they've known you.

they brace themselves, antennas up, unconsiously looking for signs that confirm their biased suspicion that you're still the same ol' same.

these dynamics can trigger the behavior you're evolving through and pull you back into old habits and ways of thinking.

it may feel like you're not progressing.

you are, i promise.

leave space to surprise.

leave space to be surprised.

be open to others' growth.

be open to your own.

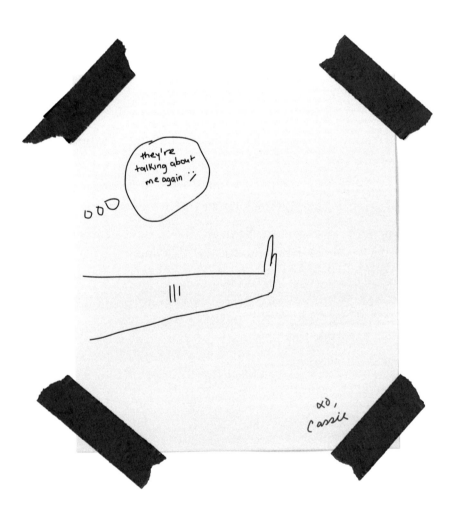

unavoidable, and that's okay.

avoid the inner circle.

they don't need your company.

if you find yourself there, back away slooooooowly, and don't make any sudden movements.

honesty and vulnerability convert insecurity into power, defensiveness into sweet surrender.

when weakness is brought to light, it loses its control. you've named it, and now you know its composition.

you are a masterful artist, an astounding designer. you turn brokenness into beauty and renew the decrepit.

chapter 4
PEACE

find your calm.

claim your piece of peace.

daily.

it's waiting for you in the last place you left it.

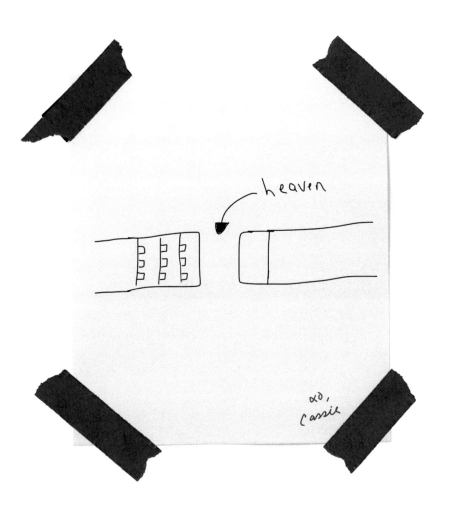

joy dwells in the mundane.

beauty hides in the nook of routine.

it's quiet and unassuming.

blink and you could miss it.

gratitude keeps your eyes wide open.

you start each day with a finite amount of energy.

shit happens.

be aware of what (and who) gets the privilege of your energy.

recharge as necessary.

laughter is food for the soul.

do it often.

sometimes loudly.

sometimes inappropriately.

sometimes to tears.

always joyously.

recharge daily, or it won't be pretty.

[insert sound of screaming woman from horror film here.]

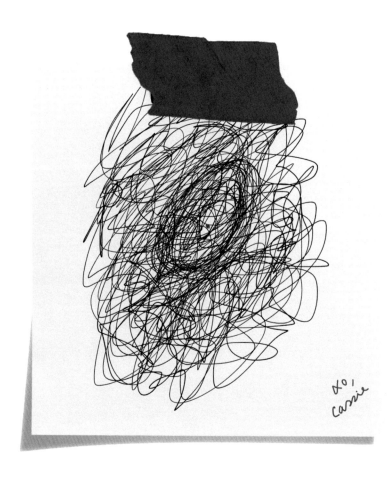

find your center through the chaos.

stay there as long as you can.

return often.

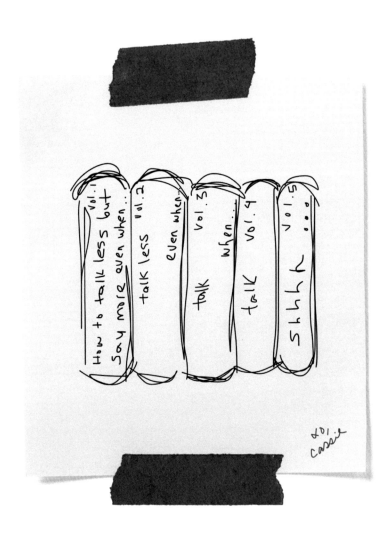

quiet. it's a gift.

less is the more you're looking for.

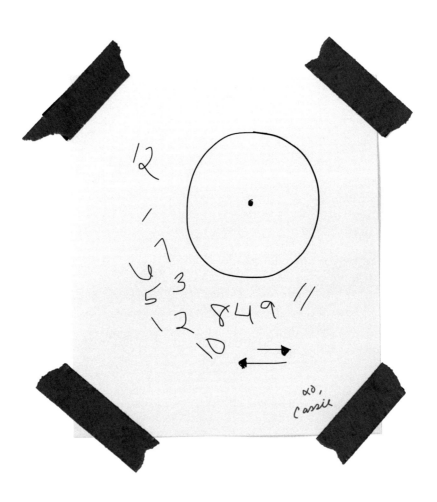

slow down.

enough.

to see.

time is relative.

so many things can get in the way of warm, nourishing and sustaining peace.

ego offers a false sense of protection from the downpour.

it also blocks the view.

sometimes it's the only sweet relief that will do.

it's an orientation.

it's a disposition.

it's a prayer.

it's a choice.

let your code of conduct be peace and love.

in the frantic energy, honey, be unmoved.

if only i could snuggle up with a day of the week.

sunday, you have mad game.

chapter 5
GOALS

fail and start again.

learn and start again.

listen and start again.

find the *art* in *start*.

there's life in a deadline.

a target to focus upon.

life always happens to a timeline.

it can be a pushy little brat.

adjust. recalibrate. listen for the *ding*.

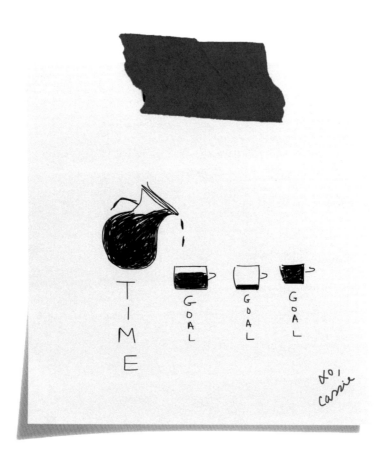

pour into what and who's important to you.

consistently.

intentionally.

you are time personified.

you are precious.

so many goals to achieve.

so many new habits to form.

impossible to do it all.

prioritize the goal that can set everything else in motion.

you ambitious beast you.

if a tree falls in a forest and no one hears, did it fall?

hell yeah, it sure did!

actions done without an audience matter.

you are your best audience.

do it for you, first and last.

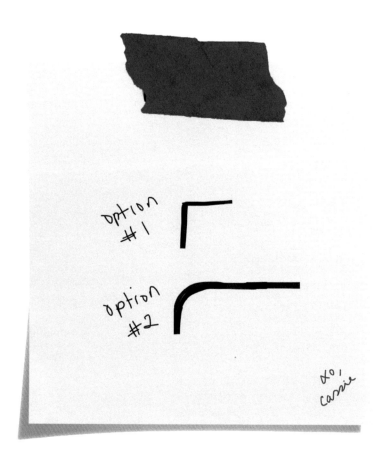

sustainable change isn't a sharp, swift right turn.

it's a slow curve. a bend made from a collection of decisions over time.

discipline and intention are the steering wheel.

every decision, no matter how small, that is made in the direction of the maximized and woke version of you has value.

the big wins are just a collection of the small ones.

celebrate those itty-bitty, microscopic, barely there wins.

they're kind of a big deal, okay?

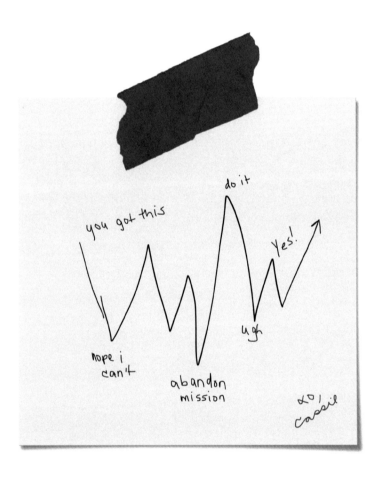

i'm of two minds, living a double life.

human + being.

beauty and challenge on both sides.

if it were easy, then there'd be nothing to write about.

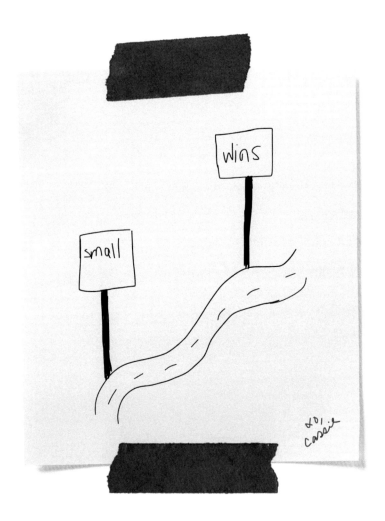

the space between *small* and *wins* is where patience resides.

get cozy there.

small does actually win, so you can keep dreaming big.

the size
of my
bag

the lunch
I forgot!

(drawn to scale)

xo,
Cassie

sometimes there will just be days when your best intentions, plans, and preparations fall short.

oops.

try again.

you're doing human perfectly.

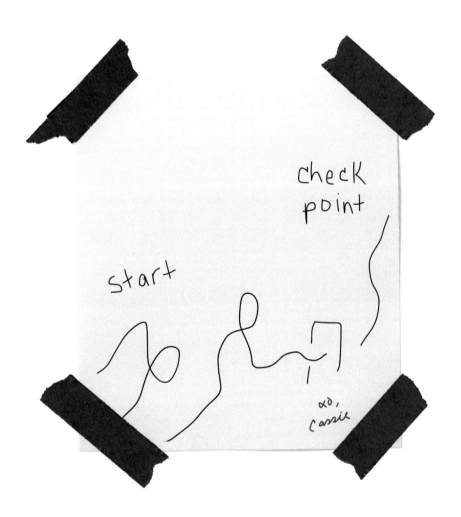

the journey from here to there is whirly and wild and perfectly made for you.

you were perfectly made
for it.

chapter 6
YOU

babe,
you're pure
magic.

xo,
Cassie

tell me you knew!

support her.

always.

be on your own damn side.

don't abandon yourself.

you're dope.

you're worthy of your own friendship.

sink deeply into you.

anchor yourself to the truth.

switch it up.
surprise yourself.
try something new.
darling, *flirt with life.*
it's yours.

don't apologize for the space you take up.

what you have to say is valuable.

your thoughts matter.

hold space fully.

sink into the moment. the moments.

own. it.

that's all this girl has to do.

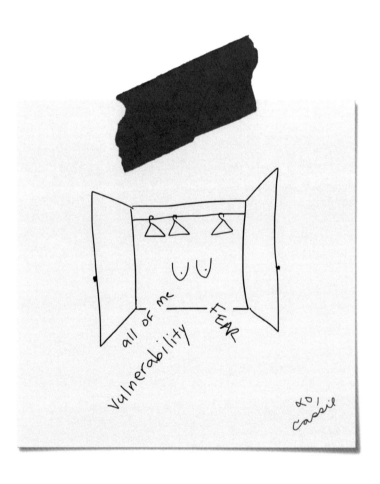

let it all hang out.

let them puppies swing.

be free to be you.

be scared and be you anyway.

yes to celebrating you.

no to needing permission.

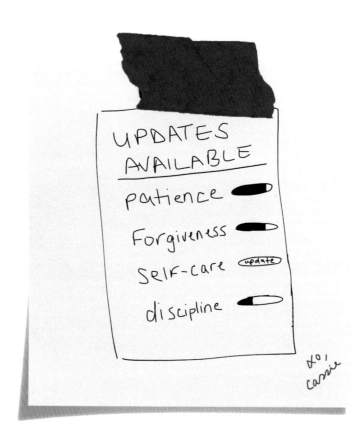

your operating system has daily updates.

the world may not always notice the progress.

you should.

you're so damn lovable.

fact!

words.

have.

matter.

for—in favor of

give—to transfer, hand over

ness—state of being

in favor of transferring to a different state of being.

com—together

pass—to move

ion—the act or process

together, we move through the process.

have the audacity to be you. as bodacious as red lips.

oh, the courage it takes to step fully into the beautiful mess of you.

to love yourself, to love others.

flaws and differences in full view.

there's nothing more audacious than that.

kiss my flaws!

chapter 7
REPEAT

yes, it's the end of the book, but it's not the end of the story.

so what now?

1. revisit the visuals and messages that resonated with you. take pictures of your favorites, save one as the background to your phone, tear it out and put it in your journal, pin it up at your desk, and so on.
2. share and discuss this book with your crew, your tribe, your family, your coworkers or even strangers. #theessentialluxuryofyou
3. create meaningful connections. bring up the topics that were meaningful to you over coffee, dinner, or a cocktail (if you're 21 years old, of course)!
4. do something you've been wanting to do—start now, start small, just start.
5. open this book up to a random page on the days you believe the lies and need a reminder of the truth.
6. remember, we're in this together. learning, unlearning, and relearning lessons daily. we're not meant to do this solo, nope! we're created to do this in a community (it's how we're designed), so let's connect @curate.this on instagram or at www.theexperimentersstudio.com.

until then, later, babe!

xo,
cass

p.s. oh, and if you need a little inspiration of the kind of questions to ask yourself, your friends, your family and random strangers, the next few pages are just for you. they have questions on each page and space for you to write and draw the answers, feelings, and thoughts that come to mind when you read the prompts. enjoy!

realization

- what do you say to yourself about yourself? does it need a refresh?
- what do you value? how do your actions align with those values? how do they not align?
- what do you typically do when you feel insecure? what do you do when you notice someone else who's insecure or lacking confidence? do you judge, empathize, and so on?
- have you ever been the "only" in a room? what did it feel like? what does it feel like when you're around people who celebrate who you are?
- what kind of conversations do you want to have and be a part of?

growth

- sometimes we get very good at hiding in plain sight, showing only a corner of ourselves. what parts of yourself do you hide and want to share more of? why?
- what have you been taking personally that you have to shed? what have you been hiding behind? what have you been protecting yourself from?
- what do you want to do less of in order to be more of who you're made to be?
- have you ever been given a great opportunity and felt fearful about squandering the opportunity? have you ever experienced perfection paralysis—you'd rather keep the dream tucked away in your mind? what did you do to move through the fear?

peace

- what behaviors and experiences bring you the deepest sense of calm?
- how does joy show up in your life in small but meaningful ways?
- what daily practices protect your piece of peace and nourish your needs?

goals

- what would you love to try or do that you keep hitting the stop button on?
- in what ways are you a more updated version of yourself than yesterday, last week, last year (you get where i'm going with this)?

you

- can you write down at least five things you want to celebrate about yourself? *really, go ahead, i'll wait.*
- when do you dance like no one is looking? in one word, how does it make you feel?
- how do you embrace the magic of you?
- are you going at the speed of you right now? what would you do in the time meant for you?
- what do you need to forgive yourself for?
- when have you abandoned yourself? what did it feel like? what does standing with yourself mean to you? how does it look and feel?
- who do you want to be? how do you want to be? take some time to curate and design who you are, you're worth it.

cassandra campbell
stanley

...is a girl-power girl.

along with being a wellesley college
alumna, she's a native
new yorker *(from the boogie-down bronx)*
and first-generation american,
born of caribbean descent.
she's a curious gal with a passion for
learning and sharing lessons learned.
she's a lover of artistic expression,
a respecter of design, an analyzer of
the process of things, and an advocate
of unapologetically seeking
ways to surprise and delight
in your creativity.

she dared to write her debut book,
the essential luxury of you,
as a sweet act of rebellion against
the false paradigm of perfection. it
intends to serve as encouragement to
celebrate who you are, flaws and all,
and to *embrace your beautiful mess!*

@curate.this
www.theexperimentersstudio.com

graphic design | izzy goodkind